EMMANUEL JOSEPH

Cryptocurrency Chronicles: Decoding the Digital Coin

Contents

1

Chapter 1: The Dawn of Digital Currency

I n the early 21st century, the concept of money began to evolve with the advent of digital currency. The financial landscape, long dominated by traditional banks and physical cash, started to see a new player: cryptocurrency. This novel form of money was decentralized, meaning it was not controlled by any single entity or government. Bitcoin, introduced by an anonymous figure known as Satoshi Nakamoto, was the first cryptocurrency to gain significant attention and laid the foundation for a new era in finance.

Bitcoin's creation was rooted in the desire for a decentralized financial system, free from the control of traditional banking institutions. It employed a revolutionary technology called blockchain, a distributed ledger that recorded transactions across a network of computers. This ensured transparency and security, as every transaction was visible to the entire network and could not be altered once confirmed. The concept of mining, where individuals used computational power to solve complex puzzles and validate transactions, was introduced, incentivizing participation and ensuring the network's integrity.

The launch of Bitcoin in 2009 was met with skepticism and curiosity. Early adopters were primarily tech enthusiasts who saw the potential for a decentralized currency. Over time, as more people became aware of Bitcoin and its underlying technology, its value began to rise. What started as a niche interest soon became a global phenomenon, with individuals and businesses exploring the possibilities of this new financial frontier.

As Bitcoin gained popularity, other cryptocurrencies emerged, each with its unique features and purposes. Ethereum, introduced in 2015, expanded on Bitcoin's concept by introducing smart contracts, self-executing contracts with the terms of the agreement directly written into code. This innovation opened the door to a myriad of applications beyond simple transactions, such as decentralized applications (dApps) and initial coin offerings (ICOs). The cryptocurrency landscape was rapidly evolving, setting the stage for a transformative shift in the way we think about and use money.

2

Chapter 2: The Mechanics of Blockchain

Blockchain technology is the backbone of cryptocurrency, providing the framework that allows for decentralized, secure, and transparent transactions. At its core, a blockchain is a digital ledger of transactions, duplicated and distributed across a network of computer systems. Each block in the chain contains a list of transactions, and every time a new transaction occurs, it is recorded on a block and added to the chain.

One of the key features of blockchain is its immutability. Once a transaction is recorded on the blockchain, it cannot be altered or deleted. This is achieved through cryptographic hashing, a process that transforms transaction data into a fixed-size string of characters, known as a hash. Each block contains the hash of the previous block, creating a chain of interlinked blocks. If any data in a block is altered, the hash changes, breaking the chain and alerting the network to the tampering attempt.

Another important aspect of blockchain is its decentralized nature. Unlike traditional centralized systems, where a single entity controls the ledger, blockchain relies on a network of nodes, each maintaining a copy of the ledger. Transactions are validated through a consensus mechanism, such as Proof of Work (PoW) or Proof of Stake (PoS), ensuring that no single entity can control or manipulate the network. This decentralization enhances security and resilience, as there is no central point of failure.

Blockchain's transparency and security have far-reaching implications beyond cryptocurrency. It has the potential to revolutionize various industries, including supply chain management, healthcare, and voting systems. By providing a tamper-proof record of transactions, blockchain can increase trust and efficiency in processes that rely on accurate and verifiable data. As the technology continues to evolve, new applications and use cases are likely to emerge, further solidifying blockchain's role in the digital age.

3

Chapter 3: The Rise of Altcoins

Following the success of Bitcoin, a plethora of alternative cryptocurrencies, commonly known as altcoins, began to emerge. These digital coins sought to address various limitations of Bitcoin and introduced innovative features and functionalities. Some altcoins focused on improving transaction speed and scalability, while others aimed to enhance privacy and anonymity. Each altcoin brought something unique to the table, contributing to the diversification and growth of the cryptocurrency ecosystem.

One of the most notable altcoins is Litecoin, created by Charlie Lee in 2011. Often referred to as the silver to Bitcoin's gold, Litecoin aimed to provide faster transaction times and lower fees. By adopting a different hashing algorithm and reducing the block generation time, Litecoin offered a more efficient and accessible alternative to Bitcoin. Over the years, it has gained a loyal following and remains one of the most widely used cryptocurrencies.

Another significant altcoin is Monero, launched in 2014 with a focus on privacy and anonymity. Unlike Bitcoin, where transactions are publicly visible on the blockchain, Monero uses advanced cryptographic techniques to obfuscate transaction details. This ensures that the sender, receiver, and transaction amount remain confidential, making Monero a popular choice for users who prioritize privacy. The development of privacy-focused altcoins highlights the diverse needs and preferences within the cryptocurrency community.

Ethereum, introduced by Vitalik Buterin in 2015, revolutionized the cryptocurrency space by introducing smart contracts and decentralized applications (dApps). While Bitcoin was designed primarily as a digital currency, Ethereum provided a platform for developers to build and deploy decentralized applications. This innovation opened up a world of possibilities, from decentralized finance (DeFi) to non-fungible tokens (NFTs), and positioned Ethereum as a leading force in the blockchain space.

The rise of altcoins has led to a vibrant and dynamic cryptocurrency market, with thousands of digital currencies available for trading and investment. Each altcoin offers unique features and use cases, catering to different needs and preferences. As the cryptocurrency ecosystem continues to evolve, new altcoins will likely emerge, further enriching the landscape and driving innovation in the digital economy.

4

Chapter 4: The ICO Boom and Bust

The advent of Initial Coin Offerings (ICOs) brought a new wave of excitement and opportunity to the cryptocurrency space. ICOs allowed startups to raise funds by issuing their own tokens in exchange for established cryptocurrencies like Bitcoin and Ethereum. This crowdfunding model bypassed traditional venture capital routes and provided a way for projects to gain traction and support from a global audience. The promise of high returns and the democratization of investment attracted a flood of participants, leading to a boom in ICO activity.

During the ICO boom of 2017, numerous projects raised substantial amounts of capital, with some reaching hundreds of millions of dollars in a matter of days. The allure of potentially groundbreaking technologies and the fear of missing out (FOMO) drove investors to pour money into ICOs, often with little due diligence. While some projects delivered on their promises and contributed to the advancement of blockchain technology, others turned out to be scams or failed to achieve their objectives.

The unregulated nature of ICOs made them a fertile ground for fraudulent activities and speculative bubbles. As the hype around ICOs grew, so did the number of dubious projects that sought to exploit investors' enthusiasm. These scams and failures led to significant financial losses for many participants and eroded trust in the ICO model. Regulatory authorities around the world began to take notice, implementing measures to protect investors and ensure transparency in fundraising activities.

The ICO bust that followed the boom served as a wake-up call for the cryptocurrency community. It highlighted the importance of thorough research and due diligence before investing in any project. The lessons learned from the ICO craze paved the way for more structured and regulated fundraising methods, such as Security Token Offerings (STOs) and Initial Exchange Offerings (IEOs). These new models aimed to address the shortcomings of ICOs and provide a more secure and compliant framework for raising capital in the cryptocurrency space.

5

Chapter 5: Decentralized Finance (DeFi)

Decentralized Finance, or DeFi, is a rapidly growing sector within the cryptocurrency space that aims to recreate and improve traditional financial systems using blockchain technology. DeFi applications leverage smart contracts to automate and execute financial transactions without the need for intermediaries like banks or brokers. This democratization of finance enables anyone with an internet connection to access a wide range of financial services, including lending, borrowing, trading, and earning interest on their assets.

One of the key components of DeFi is decentralized exchanges (DEXs), which allow users to trade cryptocurrencies directly with one another without relying on a centralized authority. DEXs operate using smart contracts, ensuring that trades are executed securely and transparently. Popular DEXs like Uniswap and SushiSwap have gained significant traction, offering users a more open and inclusive trading environment compared to traditional exchanges.

Lending and borrowing platforms are another major aspect of DeFi. These platforms enable users to lend their assets to others in exchange for interest or borrow assets by providing collateral. By eliminating intermediaries, DeFi lending platforms offer more competitive interest rates and greater flexibility. Aave and Compound are two prominent examples of DeFi lending protocols that have garnered widespread adoption and contributed to the growth of the sector.

Yield farming, or liquidity mining, is a unique innovation within DeFi that allows users to earn rewards by providing liquidity to decentralized protocols. Participants supply their assets to liquidity pools and, in return, receive tokens or interest as compensation. This mechanism incentivizes users to contribute to the liquidity and stability of DeFi platforms, fostering a more vibrant and resilient ecosystem. However, yield farming also comes with risks, such as impermanent loss and smart contract vulnerabilities, which participants must carefully consider.

The rise of DeFi has introduced a new era of financial innovation, with the potential to disrupt traditional banking and financial services. By leveraging the power of blockchain and smart contracts, DeFi offers greater accessibility, transparency, and efficiency in financial transactions. As the sector continues to evolve, it will likely play a pivotal role in shaping the future of finance, providing new opportunities and challenges for participants and regulators alike.

6

Chapter 6: The Crypto Regulatory Landscape

As cryptocurrencies gained popularity and mainstream adoption, governments and regulatory bodies around the world began to take notice. The rapid growth of the crypto market presented both opportunities and challenges, prompting regulators to establish frameworks to protect investors, prevent fraud, and ensure compliance with existing financial laws. The regulatory landscape for cryptocurrencies varies widely across different jurisdictions, reflecting the diverse approaches and perspectives of governments.

In some countries, cryptocurrencies have been embraced with open arms, with regulators working to create a supportive environment for innovation and growth. For instance, Japan has established clear guidelines for the operation of cryptocurrency exchanges and recognizes Bitcoin as a legal method of payment. This regulatory clarity has fostered a thriving crypto ecosystem, attracting businesses and investors to the country.

Conversely, other countries have taken a more cautious or restrictive approach to cryptocurrencies. China, for example, has implemented a series of measures to curb crypto activities, including banning Initial Coin Offerings (ICOs) and shutting down domestic exchanges. The Chinese government has also expressed concerns about the potential use of cryptocurrencies for illegal activities such as money laundering and tax evasion, leading to stricter regulations and increased scrutiny.

The United States has adopted a somewhat fragmented regulatory approach, with different agencies overseeing various aspects of the crypto market. The Securities and Exchange Commission (SEC) has focused on regulating ICOs and ensuring that crypto projects comply with securities laws. The Commodity Futures Trading Commission (CFTC) oversees crypto derivatives markets, while the Financial Crimes Enforcement Network (FinCEN) addresses anti-money laundering (AML) and know-your-customer (KYC) requirements. This patchwork of regulations can be challenging for businesses and investors to navigate, but it also reflects the complexity and evolving nature of the crypto space.

As the global regulatory landscape continues to develop, striking a balance between fostering innovation and ensuring investor protection remains a key challenge. Clear and consistent regulations can help build trust and confidence in the cryptocurrency market, encouraging broader adoption and integration into the traditional financial system. Collaboration between governments, industry stakeholders, and regulatory bodies will be essential in shaping the future of crypto regulation and creating a sustainable environment for growth and innovation.

7

Chapter 7: The Environmental Impact of Crypto Mining

The environmental impact of cryptocurrency mining has become a topic of growing concern and debate. Mining, particularly for cryptocurrencies like Bitcoin, requires significant computational power and energy consumption. As miners compete to solve complex mathematical puzzles and validate transactions, they use powerful hardware that consumes vast amounts of electricity. This energy-intensive process has raised questions about the sustainability and environmental footprint of the crypto industry.

Bitcoin mining, in particular, has been criticized for its high energy consumption. Studies have estimated that the Bitcoin network's energy usage rivals that of some small countries, leading to concerns about its contribution to carbon emissions and climate change. The majority of Bitcoin mining operations are concentrated in regions with cheap electricity, often generated from fossil fuels like coal, further exacerbating the environmental impact.

In response to these concerns, some initiatives and projects have emerged to promote more sustainable and eco-friendly mining practices. One approach is the use of renewable energy sources, such as solar, wind, and hydroelectric power, to fuel mining operations. By tapping into cleaner energy alternatives, miners can reduce their carbon footprint and mitigate the environmental impact of their activities. Some mining farms have already begun to transition to renewable energy, setting an example for others to follow.

Another potential solution is the development and adoption of more energy-efficient consensus mechanisms. While Bitcoin relies on the energy-intensive Proof of Work (PoW) algorithm, other cryptocurrencies have explored alternatives like Proof of Stake (PoS) and Delegated Proof of Stake (DPoS). These consensus mechanisms require significantly less energy to operate, as they do not involve the same level of computational competition. Ethereum, for example, is in the process of transitioning from PoW to PoS through its Ethereum 2.0 upgrade, aiming to achieve greater scalability and energy efficiency.

The environmental impact of crypto mining is a complex issue that requires ongoing attention and innovation. As the industry continues to grow, finding sustainable solutions will be crucial in addressing environmental concerns and ensuring the long-term viability of cryptocurrencies. By embracing renewable energy, developing energy-efficient technologies, and raising awareness about the environmental implications of mining, the crypto community can work towards a more sustainable future.

8

Chapter 8: Security and Privacy in the Crypto World

S
ecurity and privacy are paramount concerns in the world of
cryptocurrencies. The decentralized and digital nature of crypto
assets presents unique challenges and vulnerabilities that require
robust measures to protect users and their funds. As the value and adoption
of cryptocurrencies have increased, so too have the threats from hackers,
scammers, and other malicious actors seeking to exploit weaknesses in the
system.

One of the primary security risks in the crypto world is the potential
for hacking and theft. Cryptocurrency exchanges, where users buy, sell,
and store their digital assets, have been frequent targets of cyberattacks.
High-profile exchange hacks, such as the Mt. Gox incident in 2014 and
the Coincheck hack in 2018, resulted in the loss of hundreds of millions
of dollars' worth of cryptocurrencies. These incidents underscore the
importance of implementing robust security measures, including multi-factor
authentication, cold storage, and regular security audits, to protect users'
funds.

In addition to exchange hacks, individual users must also be vigilant
about securing their own crypto wallets. Wallets are digital tools that store
users' private keys, which are necessary for accessing and managing their

cryptocurrencies. If a private key is lost or stolen, the corresponding funds can be irretrievably lost. To mitigate this risk, users are advised to use hardware wallets, which are physical devices that store private keys offline, and to keep backups of their keys in secure locations.

Privacy is another critical consideration for cryptocurrency users. While blockchain transactions are transparent and publicly visible, they are also pseudonymous, meaning that users' identities are not directly linked to their addresses. However, with enough data and analysis, it is possible to trace transactions and potentially identify users. Privacy-focused cryptocurrencies, such as Monero and Zcash, have been developed to address these concerns by implementing advanced cryptographic techniques that obfuscate transaction details and enhance user anonymity.

Despite the challenges, the crypto community continues to innovate and develop new solutions to enhance security and privacy. Projects focused on secure multi-party computation, zero-knowledge proofs, and decentralized identity management are exploring ways to protect users' data and assets. By prioritizing security and privacy, the crypto world can build trust and confidence, fostering wider adoption and acceptance of digital currencies.

Chapter 9: The Future of Cryptocurrencies

T he future of cryptocurrencies is a topic of much speculation and excitement. As the technology and market continue to evolve, several trends and developments are likely to shape the trajectory of the crypto landscape. From increased mainstream adoption to technological advancements and regulatory changes, the future holds both opportunities and challenges for cryptocurrencies and their users.

One of the most significant trends is the growing acceptance and integration of cryptocurrencies into traditional financial systems and everyday life. Major financial institutions, payment processors, and technology companies are increasingly exploring ways to incorporate digital currencies into their services. For example, companies like PayPal and Square have enabled cryptocurrency transactions on their platforms, making it easier for users to buy, sell, and use digital assets. This mainstream adoption is expected to drive further growth and acceptance of cryptocurrencies as a legitimate form of money.

Technological advancements will also play a crucial role in shaping the future of cryptocurrencies. Innovations in blockchain scalability, interoperability, and security will address some of the current limitations and challenges faced by crypto networks. The development of Layer 2 solutions, such as the Lightning Network for Bitcoin and Plasma for Ethereum, aims to improve transaction speeds and reduce fees, making cryptocurrencies more practical for everyday use. Additionally, advancements in privacy technologies and decentralized applications (dApps) will open up new possibilities and use cases for digital currencies.

Regulation will continue to be a key factor influencing the future of cryptocurrencies. As governments and regulatory bodies establish clearer guidelines and frameworks, the crypto market is likely to become more stable and secure. Regulation can help protect investors, prevent fraud, and promote transparency, fostering greater trust and confidence in the crypto ecosystem. However, finding the right balance between innovation and regulation will be crucial to avoid stifling growth and creativity.

The rise of central bank digital currencies (CBDCs) is another development that could impact the future of cryptocurrencies. CBDCs are digital versions of traditional fiat currencies issued and controlled by central banks. Several countries, including China and Sweden, are actively exploring and piloting CBDC projects. While CBDCs could enhance the efficiency and security of payment systems, they also raise questions about privacy and the potential displacement of existing cryptocurrencies. The coexistence and interaction between CBDCs and decentralized cryptocurrencies will be an area of significant interest and research in the coming years.

10

Chapter 10: NFTs and the Digital Art Revolution

Non-fungible tokens (NFTs) have emerged as one of the most transformative innovations in the cryptocurrency space, particularly in the realm of digital art and collectibles. Unlike traditional cryptocurrencies, which are fungible and interchangeable, NFTs represent unique digital assets that can be bought, sold, and traded on blockchain platforms. Each NFT is distinct and verifiable, thanks to the use of blockchain technology, making it an ideal medium for representing ownership of digital art, music, videos, and other creative works.

The rise of NFTs has revolutionized the digital art world, providing artists with new opportunities to monetize their creations and reach global audiences. By minting their work as NFTs, artists can retain ownership and control over their digital assets while benefiting from the transparency and security of blockchain. NFTs also enable artists to earn royalties on secondary sales, ensuring that they continue to profit from their work as it changes hands in the marketplace. This newfound ability to track and authenticate digital art has led to an explosion of creativity and innovation in the art community.

One of the most high-profile NFT sales was the auction of Beeple's digital artwork "Everydays: The First 5000 Days" at Christie's in March 2021. The piece sold for a staggering $69 million, catapulting NFTs into the mainstream spotlight and sparking widespread interest in the potential of digital art. This landmark event demonstrated the value and legitimacy of NFTs as a new asset class and highlighted the growing acceptance of digital art within traditional art markets.

Beyond digital art, NFTs have found applications in various other domains, including gaming, virtual real estate, and sports memorabilia. In the gaming industry, NFTs are used to represent in-game assets, such as characters, items, and skins, allowing players to truly own and trade their virtual possessions. Virtual worlds like Decentraland and The Sandbox use NFTs to enable the purchase and development of virtual land, creating immersive and interactive digital environments. Sports organizations and athletes have also embraced NFTs to create digital collectibles, such as trading cards and highlight reels, providing fans with unique and verifiable memorabilia.

The NFT phenomenon has opened up new possibilities for creators and collectors alike, bridging the gap between the physical and digital worlds. As the technology continues to evolve, it is likely that we will see even more innovative and diverse applications of NFTs, further blurring the lines between reality and the digital realm.

11

Chapter 11: Cryptocurrencies in Emerging Markets

C ryptocurrencies have had a profound impact on emerging markets, offering new opportunities for financial inclusion, economic growth, and innovation. In regions where traditional banking infrastructure is limited or unreliable, cryptocurrencies provide an alternative means of accessing financial services and participating in the global economy. This has been particularly beneficial for individuals and businesses in developing countries, who can now leverage digital currencies to overcome barriers and improve their financial well-being.

One of the key advantages of cryptocurrencies in emerging markets is their ability to facilitate cross-border transactions and remittances. Traditional remittance services are often costly and slow, with fees and delays cutting into the funds sent to recipients. Cryptocurrencies, on the other hand, enable fast and low-cost transfers, allowing individuals to send money to their families and friends with minimal friction. This has the potential to significantly improve the livelihoods of people in countries that rely heavily on remittances, such as the Philippines, Nigeria, and El Salvador.

In addition to remittances, cryptocurrencies have also enabled greater financial inclusion by providing access to banking services for the unbanked and underbanked populations. In many developing countries, a significant portion of the population lacks access to traditional banking services due to factors such as distance, cost, and lack of documentation. Cryptocurrencies and mobile wallets offer a more accessible and affordable alternative, allowing people to store, send, and receive money securely using their smartphones. This has empowered individuals to participate in the digital economy and access services that were previously out of reach.

Emerging markets have also seen a surge in entrepreneurial activity and innovation driven by cryptocurrencies and blockchain technology. Startups and small businesses in these regions are leveraging digital currencies to raise capital, streamline operations, and expand their reach. Blockchain-based solutions are being developed to address various challenges, such as supply chain transparency, land registry, and identity verification. By harnessing the power of cryptocurrencies, emerging markets have the potential to leapfrog traditional financial systems and drive sustainable economic growth.

However, the adoption of cryptocurrencies in emerging markets is not without challenges. Issues such as regulatory uncertainty, volatility, and lack of digital literacy can pose significant hurdles. Governments and stakeholders must work together to create supportive environments that foster innovation while protecting consumers and ensuring the stability of the financial system. By addressing these challenges, cryptocurrencies can play a pivotal role in unlocking the full potential of emerging markets and driving inclusive growth and development.

12

Chapter 12: The Social Impact of Cryptocurrencies

The social impact of cryptocurrencies extends beyond the realm of finance, influencing various aspects of society and human interaction. As digital currencies become more integrated into our daily lives, they have the potential to drive significant social change, promoting transparency, empowerment, and inclusivity. From philanthropy and charitable giving to social movements and community building, cryptocurrencies are reshaping the way we connect, collaborate, and support one another.

One of the most promising social applications of cryptocurrencies is in the area of philanthropy and charitable giving. Cryptocurrencies enable donors to contribute funds directly to causes and organizations without the need for intermediaries, ensuring that a greater portion of donations reaches those in need. Blockchain technology also provides transparency and accountability, allowing donors to track their contributions and see how they are being used. This has the potential to increase trust and engagement in charitable efforts, encouraging more people to give and support important causes.

Social movements and advocacy groups have also embraced cryptocurrencies as a means of raising funds and mobilizing supporters. Digital currencies provide a way for activists to bypass traditional financial systems and access resources independently, making it easier to organize and sustain grassroots campaigns. For example, during times of political unrest or economic instability, cryptocurrencies can offer a lifeline for individuals and groups facing financial censorship or restrictions. By facilitating access to funds and resources, cryptocurrencies empower communities to advocate for change and address social injustices.

In addition to philanthropy and activism, cryptocurrencies have the potential to promote financial literacy and empowerment. As individuals learn to navigate the world of digital currencies, they gain valuable skills and knowledge that can help them make informed financial decisions. This increased awareness and understanding of financial concepts can lead to greater economic independence and resilience, particularly for marginalized and underserved populations. Educational initiatives and programs that focus on cryptocurrency and blockchain technology can play a crucial role in bridging the digital divide and fostering a more inclusive society.

Furthermore, the decentralized nature of cryptocurrencies encourages the development of new forms of governance and collaboration. Decentralized autonomous organizations (DAOs) are one such innovation, allowing communities to come together and make collective decisions without the need for centralized authority. DAOs operate through smart contracts, enabling members to propose, vote on, and execute actions transparently and democratically. This model of decentralized governance has the potential to transform various aspects of society, from business and finance to social and political organizations.

As cryptocurrencies continue to evolve and gain traction, their social impact will become increasingly evident. By promoting transparency, empowerment, and inclusivity, digital currencies have the potential to drive positive change and contribute to a more equitable and just world. The future of cryptocurrencies is not only about technological advancements and financial innovation but also about the ways in which they can improve our lives and strengthen our communities.

www.ingramcontent.com/pod-product-compliance
Lightning Source LLC
Chambersburg PA
CBHW070929050326
40689CB00015B/3677